A  **TRUE** BOOK™

Incredible Plants!

Plants and Ecosystems

Alexa Kurzius

Children's Press®
An Imprint of Scholastic Inc.

Content Consultant
Michael Freeling, PhD
Professor
Department of Plant & Microbial Biology
University of California, Berkeley
Berkeley, California

Library of Congress Cataloging-in-Publication Data
Names: Kurzius, Alexa, author.
Title: Plants and ecosystems / by Alexa Kurzius.
Description: New York, NY : Children's Press, an imprint of Scholastic Inc., 2020. | Series: A true book |
    Includes bibliographical references and index.
Identifiers: LCCN 2019004804 | ISBN 9780531234648 (library binding) | ISBN 9780531240076
    (paperback)
Subjects: LCSH: Plant ecology—Juvenile literature.
Classification: LCC QK901 .K87 2020 | DDC 581.7—dc23
LC record available at https://lccn.loc.gov/2019004804

All rights reserved. Published in 2020 by Children's Press, an imprint of Scholastic Inc.
Printed in China 62

SCHOLASTIC, CHILDREN'S PRESS, A TRUE BOOK™, and associated logos are trademarks and/or
registered trademarks of Scholastic Inc.

Scholastic Inc., 557 Broadway, New York, NY 10012

1 2 3 4 5 6 7 8 9 10 R 29 28 27 26 25 24 23 22 21 20

**Front cover: A forested area in
Mauritius in the Indian Ocean**

Back cover: Arctic cotton grass

Find the Truth!

Everything you are about to read is true *except* for one of the sentences on this page.

Which one is **TRUE**?

T or F The tundra has short winters and long summers.

T or F Climate change affects ecosystems.

Find the answers in this book.

3

Contents

The **BIG** Truth

Ecosystems and Climate Change

Orchids

Flowering cacti

3 Desert, Taiga, and Tundra

What is life like in some of the world's most
extreme biomes?. 31

4 In the Water

How do water biomes vary from
those on land? 39

Levels of the
rain forest

Think About It!

Take a close look at the photo on these pages. What kinds of foods do you think these animals eat? Believe it or not, some of the world's biggest animals eat nothing but plants. Plants provide energy and nutrients to countless **species** around the world. But where do they get this energy? Plants don't consume other plants. So what do they eat to survive?

Stumped?
Want to know more? Turn the page!

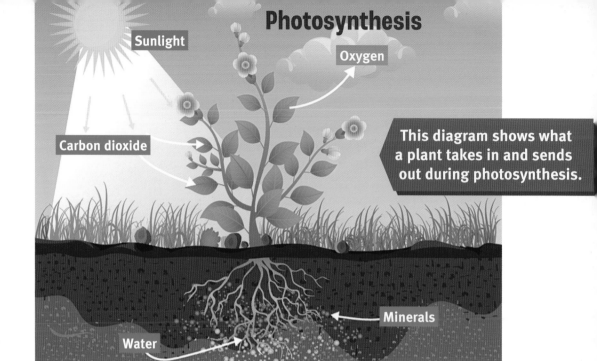

Photosynthesis

Sunlight

Oxygen

Carbon dioxide

This diagram shows what a plant takes in and sends out during photosynthesis.

Minerals

Water

If you guessed that plants make their own food, you are right! Plants do not eat food the same way humans and other animals do. Instead, they survive and grow through a process called photosynthesis. During photosynthesis, a plant's roots pull water and minerals from the soil. The plant also absorbs carbon dioxide from the air. Using the energy in sunlight, photosynthesis combines the water and carbon dioxide into food.

Plants are an essential part of every **ecosystem**. Humans and other animals enjoy the food that plants produce. Even animals that don't directly eat plants depend on meat from plant-eating species. Plants also release oxygen into the air as a by-product of photosynthesis. Animals rely on this oxygen to breathe. In addition, plants help maintain our planet's **climate**. The world as we know it could not exist without plants!

There are about 400,000 species of plants on Earth!

Forests cover about one-third of Earth's land.

Humans are part of a biological community that includes plants, animals, and microoganisms.

Ecosystems and Biomes

Earth is full of life. Even places that seem empty at first glance could be packed with thousands of plants, animals, and **microorganisms**. All the species in any given area live together in a biological community. This community is called an ecosystem. Ecosystems exist all over the world. An ecosystem can be as small as a tiny pond or as large as an entire continent. Larger ecosystems are made up of many smaller ones.

Elephants help plants grow in an ecosystem by spreading seeds through their droppings.

A Biological Community

All ecosystems are made up of living and nonliving things. Living things in an ecosystem are called biotic factors. They include plants, animals, and microorganisms. Each biotic factor is found in its own habitat. This is a specific place within an ecosystem.

Nonliving things are called abiotic factors. These include sunlight, soil, water, and carbon dioxide. All living things need abiotic factors to survive.

The Plant Kingdom

In the 1700s, Swedish scientist Carl Linnaeus began a project to organize all living things. He grouped everything into two categories called kingdoms: the animal kingdom and the plant kingdom.

Plants are a group of organisms made up of more than one cell. Most plants go through photosynthesis. Some plants have leaves, roots, stems, and seeds. Others do not.

Today, scientists often divide living things into six kingdoms. They include plants (pictured), animals, bacteria, bacteria-like organisms, fungi, and protists.

Helping Each Other Out

Plants do much more for animals than just provide a source of food. Many animals use plants for shelter. Birds build nests from twigs. Squirrels raise their young inside of hollow trees.

In return, animals can be useful to plants. Some animals help spread plant seeds. Others help flowering plants reproduce by spreading their pollen. These kinds of relationships are known as symbiosis. The symbiotic relationship generally benefits all the organisms involved.

Many animals eat fruits and flowers produced by plants.

The roots of mangrove trees help prevent erosion in coastal regions near the equator.

Supporting the Soil

Plants can also improve the quality of abiotic factors in an ecosystem. Plant roots help protect soil from **erosion**. They strengthen the soil so it cannot be washed away easily. Plants can even continue to help improve the quality of soil after they die. As dead plants break down, they add nutrients back into the soil. Then other plants absorb these nutrients, which helps them grow.

Links in a Chain

In an ecosystem, energy and nutrients are passed among living things in a food web.

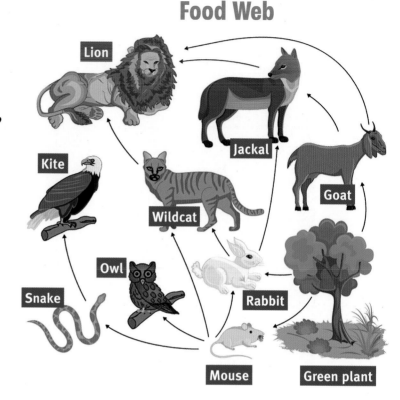

Food Web

Lion

Jackal

Kite

Wildcat

Goat

Owl

Snake

Rabbit

Mouse

Green plant

Different organisms play different roles in the web. Some, such as plants, produce energy using photosynthesis. Other organisms get their energy from eating these **producers**. This forms a complex web of organisms that produce energy and consume one another. If any species is removed from an ecosystem, the entire food web is affected.

Energy Flow in an Ecosystem

Here's an example of how energy flows within an ecosystem on land:

PRODUCERS: Plants are producers. They use abiotic factors to produce energy-packed food.

producers

grass

bushes

trees

bacteria

fungi

PRIMARY CONSUMERS: Organisms that only eat plants are called primary, or first, **consumers**. These species are also known as herbivores.

herbivores

SECONDARY CONSUMERS: Organisms that eat primary consumers are secondary consumers. Some eat only meat. Others eat both meat and plants.

carnivores

worms

DECOMPOSERS: Fungi, bacteria, and some insects and snails are **decomposers**. They feed on dead animals and plants. This process breaks down the dead organisms and returns nutrients to the soil.

omnivorous

Biomes of the World

Large ecosystems are called **biomes**. Biomes are defined by a combination of their organisms, soil types, and climates. Different biomes can have very different features. Some are very dry. Others get rain nearly every day. Some biomes are always hot or always cold. In others, major temperature changes happen all the time. Some biomes have tall mountains. Others are wide open and flat. All these features affect the types of life found in a biome.

Scientists group the world into several major biomes.

Biomes that are similar to one another can exist in distant parts of the world. There are tropical rain forest biomes in South America, Africa, and Asia. There are deserts on nearly every continent. You can see for yourself where different kinds of biomes are located by looking at the map below. What else does this map tell you about biomes?

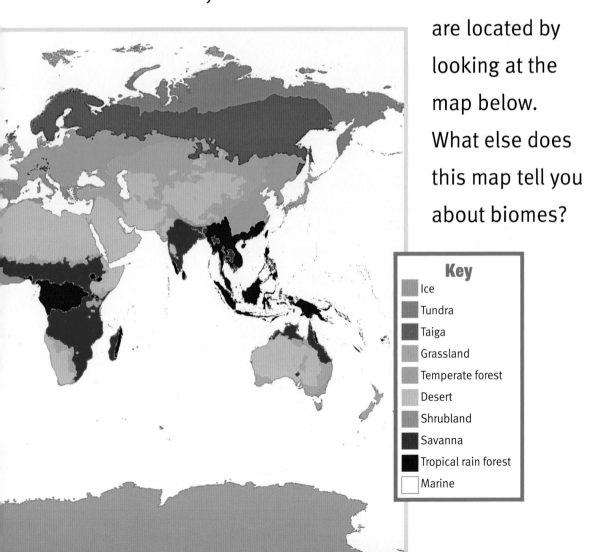

Key

Ice
Tundra
Taiga
Grassland
Temperate forest
Desert
Shrubland
Savanna
Tropical rain forest
Marine

About half of all the world's animal and plant species live in rain forests like this one in Brazil.

The first land plants appeared about 470 million years ago.

Forests and Grasslands

Forests and grasslands are some of the most diverse biomes in the world. They are home to millions of species of plants, animals, and other forms of life. For many thousands of years before European explorers and settlers landed in North America, forests and grasslands dominated the continent. But in the 1800s, settlers started clearing and farming the land at an increasing speed. This led many native species to disappear, changing local ecosystems forever.

Tropical Rain Forests

Tropical rain forest biomes cover only 6 to 7 percent of the planet. So many plants are packed into rain forests, however, that they provide much of the world's oxygen. Tropical rain forests are warm all year. They also get a lot of rain. Plant species that are very active in photosynthesis thrive in this warm, wet climate. Tropical rain forests have a wider variety of plant species than any other biome.

Tropical rain forests are located near the equator.

On average, a new species is discovered in the rain forest every two days.

The Layers of a Tropical Rain Forest

Some scientists divide tropical rain forests into four layers. Each layer is home to different organisms.

- The emergent layer is on top. It has very tall treetops that poke up above the rest of the forest.
- The layer beneath is the canopy. This dense growth of tree branches forms a roof over the bottom two layers of forest.
- The next layer is called the understory. It gets very little light because the canopy blocks most sunshine.
- The lowest layer is the forest floor. Shade-loving plants grow there as dead plant parts decay into the soil.

Emergent layer

Canopy

Understory

Forest floor

Temperate Forests

Temperate forests go through major weather changes as the seasons turn. Plants in these biomes survive both icy winters and hot summers.

Deciduous trees dominate the temperate forest biome. The leaves of these trees change color and fall off each year as the weather becomes colder. The leaves grow back in spring, when temperatures begin to rise again.

The leaves on deciduous trees change color in fall, turning forests bright red, orange, and yellow.

Unlike in rain forests, sunlight reaches all the way to the forest floor in temperate forests.

Canopy

Understory

Shrubs

Floor

The Layers of a Temperate Forest

Deciduous temperate forests have four basic layers of plant growth.

- The top layer, called the canopy, is formed from the branches of the tallest, oldest trees in the forest.

- Younger trees called saplings form the understory.

- The third layer has smaller, bushy plants called shrubs.

- Closer to the floor grow ferns, wildflowers, and herbs. Mosses and lichens grow on rocks and tree trunks.

Grasslands in the United States are often referred to as prairies.

Buffalo graze in a grassland in South Dakota.

Grasslands

Grasslands are covered in—you guessed it—plenty of grass. The land is mostly flat in this biome, and there are few trees. A variety of animals eat the wild grasses. This doesn't kill the plant. Wild grasses can grow back season after season, even after animals feed on them. The parts of these plants that are responsible for growth are located underground. Animals would get a mouthful of dirt before they could kill a grass plant.

Savannas

A savanna is a tropical grassland biome. Its climate is warm year-round. Almost all the biome's rain falls during a period of six to eight months. For the rest of the year, there is a drought. During periods of drought, wildfires are common. These fires keep the savanna healthy. They prevent woody plants such as trees from overtaking the wild grasses. They also burn away dead plant material and return nutrients to the soil.

Savanna covers much of northern Australia.

Ecosystems and Climate Change

Ecosystems sometimes go through natural changes. But humans are causing such changes to happen much more quickly than usual. Activities such as clearing forests and burning oil, coal, and other fossil fuels are leading to global climate change. Climate change is a shift in Earth's average temperature and weather patterns. Because ecosystems rely on certain climate conditions to remain healthy, this shift poses many risks. Here are just a few examples of the dangers of climate change:

Countries like India, Pakistan, Afghanistan, and Iran are experiencing droughts more frequently.

Species Extinction

All organisms have traits that developed over a long period of time to fit their natural environments. But the environment is changing faster than organisms can change to keep up. As a result, some species have gone extinct, and many are clearly at risk. Once extinct, a species cannot return.

Gilles G. © 20

An endangered plant

More Frequent Droughts

Droughts are becoming more common in biomes where they were once rare. The effects are felt all across the food web. Many types of plants are unable to survive long periods without water. As these plants die, animals are left without food and shelter.

A forest in New Caledonia, in the South Pacific, suffering drought

Changing Air and Weather

People cut down trees to make wood and paper products and to make room for farmland. This threatens many plant and animal species. It also affects climates and air quality. Healthy rain forests absorb carbon dioxide from the air and release oxygen, as well as regulate weather patterns.

Deforestation in the Amazon, in South America

More than one billion people live in desert regions around the world.

Deserts cover almost one-fifth of the land on Earth.

Desert, Taiga, and Tundra

Some biomes are shaped by extreme conditions. Intensely hot or cold temperatures can limit which plant species survive in an ecosystem. So can a lack of rainfall. But even in the planet's most extreme locations, plants have ways to thrive. Many species in these ecosystems rely on specialized adaptations. These traits have developed over time to help plants grow in poor soil, withstand brutal weather, and more.

Hot and Dry

Desert biomes are some of the driest places on the planet. They receive less than 12 inches (30 centimeters) of rain a year. Deserts also tend to have extreme temperatures. In the deserts of the southwestern United States, daytime temperatures regularly rise above 100 degrees Fahrenheit (38 degrees Celsius). The plants there have adapted to the climate. Many desert plants have broad, shallow root systems that help them trap water. Many are also succulents, fleshy plants that store water in their thick leaves and stems.

Cacti are a type of succulent.

A Cold Desert?

Not all deserts are hot. Some are extremely cold. The coldest is in Antarctica. It is nearly always below freezing there. Though the continent is covered in ice, it doesn't snow much. What little snow does fall never melts, so it builds up over years.

Only a small number of species survive in this brutally icy biome. Tiny moss plants cling to island rocks. Small flowering plants such as Antarctic hair grass and Antarctic pearlwort grow along the continent's edges.

Moss grows on Antarctic rocks

A ship breaks through ice off the coast of Antarctica

Frozen Forests

The taiga is a cold biome that is mostly forest. It also contains grasslands, wetlands, and barren areas. Some places even have **glaciers**. Long, cold winters bring bitter winds. Summers are brief and wet, with long days.

The taiga covers much of the land north of temperate forests and south of the North Pole. Most of the world's taiga is in the region of Russia known as Siberia. The taiga also covers parts of Alaska, Canada, and Europe.

The taiga is the perfect environment for evergreen trees called conifers. Conifers produce cones, not flowers. These cones contain seeds. Conifers also have narrow, needlelike leaves that stay green all year long. The most common types of trees in the taiga include fir, pine, and spruce. Flowering deciduous trees such as birch, oak, and willow also grow in the taiga, though they are less common.

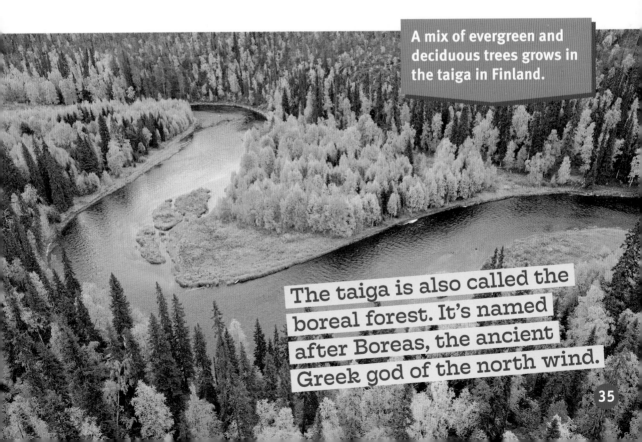

A mix of evergreen and deciduous trees grows in the taiga in Finland.

The taiga is also called the boreal forest. It's named after Boreas, the ancient Greek god of the north wind.

Arctic Tundra

The Arctic tundra biome is so cold that a layer of its soil, called permafrost, is always frozen. This biome covers the northernmost reaches of the planet. Here, summers bring rain and fog. Water gathers in ponds on the ground's surface because it cannot soak into the frozen soil. As a result, the soil has poor nutrients, and there are almost no trees. Instead, shorter plants such as mosses, grasses, and shrubs grow.

Tundra biomes have long winters and short summers.

Alpine tundra is mostly found in the Northern Hemisphere.

Alpine Tundra

The alpine tundra biome is found atop mountains around the world. Unlike Arctic tundra, it is not usually covered in permafrost. Water is able to seep into the small amount of soil here. It is still difficult, however, for trees and other tall plants to grow. This is partially because of the strong winds that blow across mountaintops. Short plants—including grasses, dwarf trees, and shrubs that stay low and cling to the ground—are better able to thrive.

The temperature in water biomes is warmest near the surface, which receives the most energy from the sun's rays.

White water lilies grow in a lake in France.

In the Water

Water biomes cover about three-fourths of the planet. Unlike land biomes, they are not defined by weather and landscape. Instead, they can be organized into freshwater and saltwater biomes. These biomes can be divided into smaller ecosystems based on several factors. Some species, for example, live only at certain depths. Other species live only in flowing waterways such as rivers and streams. Some are found only in estuaries, where salt water and fresh water blend together.

Saltwater Ecosystems

Nearly all of Earth's water is salt water. Along coasts, plants such as seagrass grow from the ocean floor. The ocean is also home to plantlike organisms called algae. Kelp and other large algae species are sometimes called seaweed. Like most plants, algae use photosynthesis to create their food. This means they play a very similar role in ecosystems to plants. Algae produce more than half the world's oxygen. They also provide food for many marine animals.

In estuaries such as Chesapeake Bay, fresh water from rivers and other bodies of water mixes with salt water from the ocean.

Water lillies grow in temperate and tropical freshwater biomes worldwide. Their flowers bloom at the surface.

Freshwater Ecosystems

Freshwater ecosystems include ponds, lakes, streams, and rivers. Like oceans, freshwater ecosystems host a variety of algae species. But a wider variety of true plants are able to grow in and around the water in these ecosystems. Some types of plants, such as water lilies, have leaves that float on the surface. Others grow completely submerged.

These and all plants are essential parts of every ecosystem on Earth. From river bottom to mountaintop, we need plants to live!

Your Own Ecosystem

You can make your own ecosystem with just a few supplies.

Directions

1 Cut the bottle into two pieces with the scissors as shown.

Materials

2-liter soda bottle with cap

Scissors

Drill or a hammer and nail

Cotton string at least 6 inches (15 cm) long

Water from a pond, stream, or puddle

Gravel

Soil

Grass seeds or seeds from another fast-growing plant

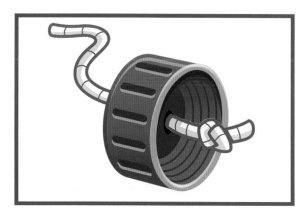

2 Ask an adult to drill or hammer a hole in the bottle cap. Thread the string halfway through the hole. Screw the cap onto the bottle.

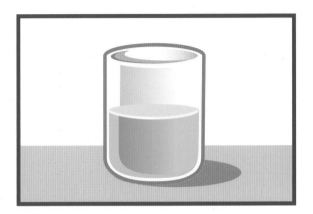

3 Fill the bottom part of the bottle halfway with the water.

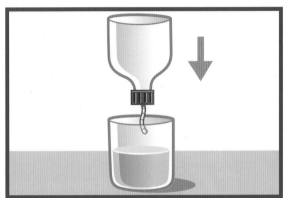

4 Place the top of the bottle upside down in the bottom part. Make sure the string reaches into the water.

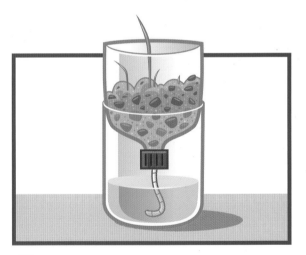

5 Add gravel, soil, and seeds to the bottle's top. Run the string up through the soil and not against the side of the bottle.

Explain It!

Place the bottle in the sun and wait a week or two. Do your plants grow? Using what you've learned in this book, can you explain what happened? If you need help, turn back to chapter 1.

True Statistics

Estimated number of plant species on the planet: 400,000

Number of known flowering plant species: 369,000

Estimated fraction of plant species that are in danger of extinction: More than 1/5

Number of plant species used in medicine: 28,200

Percentage of cancer-fighting plant species that are found in the tropical rain forest: 70

Largest land biome: Taiga

Percentage of sunlight that reaches all the way to the ground layer of the tropical rain forest: 2

Did you find the truth?

F The tundra has short winters and long summers.

T Climate change affects ecosystems.

Resources

Other books in this series:

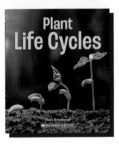

You can also look at:

Gray, Susan Heinrichs. *Ecology: The Study of Ecosystems*. New York: Children's Press, 2012.

Ignotofsky Rachel. *The Wondrous Workings of Planet Earth: Understanding Our World and Its Ecosystems*. New York: Ten Speed Press, 2018.

Latham, Donna, and Tom Casteel (illust.). *Biomes: Discover the Earth's Ecosystems with Environmental Science Activities for Kids*. White River Junction, VT: Nomad Press, 2019.

Glossary

biomes (BYE-ohmz) large community types made up of the living and nonliving elements that exist in a region

climate (KLYE-mit) the weather typical of a place over a long period of time

consumers (kuhn-SOO-murz) organisms in an ecosystem that feed on other organisms

decomposers (dee-kuhm-POH-zurz) organisms in an ecosystem that break down dead matter

ecosystem (EE-koh-sihs-tuhm) all the living things in a place and their relation to their environment

erosion (ih-ROH-zhuhn) the wearing away of something by water, wind, or other factors

glaciers (GLAY-shurz) slow-moving masses of ice formed when snow falls and does not melt because the temperature remains below freezing

microorganisms (mye-kroh-OR-guh-niz-uhmz) living things that are so small they can be seen only with a microscope

producers (pruh-DOO-surz) organisms in an ecosystem that produce their own food

species (SPEE-sheez) one of the groups into which living things are divided; members of the same species can mate and have offspring

Index

Page numbers in **bold** indicate illustrations.

About the Author

Alexa Kurzius writes and produces videos for Scholastic's elementary STEM magazines. She's been reporting since she was in the fourth grade, when she penned a picture book about penguins. She has a bachelor's degree in English and psychology and a master's degree in science journalism. She lives in New York City with her husband.